RESCUING ROVER

RESCUING ROVER

Saving America's Dogs

Raymond Bial

Houghton Mifflin
Houghton Mifflin Harcourt
Boston   New York   2011

Houghton Mifflin is an imprint of Houghton Mifflin Harcourt Publishing Company.

www.hmhbooks.com

The text of this book is set in Sabon.
Book design by Ellen Nygaard

Library of Congress Cataloging-in-Publication Data

Bial, Raymond.
  Rescuing Rover : saving America's dogs / Raymond Bial.
    p. cm.
  ISBN 978-0-547-34125-5
1. Dog rescue—United States—Juvenile literature. 2. Dogs—United States—Juvenile literature. 3. Animal rescue—United States—Juvenile literature. I. Title.
  HV4746.B53 2011
  636.08'32—dc22
2010025123

Manufactured in China
LEO 10 9 8 7 6 5 4 3 2 1
4500269707

Rescuing Rover is dedicated to all the kind people who have devoted themselves to helping dogs. They are a great inspiration to us all.

✺A✺C✺K✺N✺O✺W✺L✺E✺D✺G✺M✺E✺N✺T✺S✺

This book would not have been possible without the gracious assistance of a number of individuals and organizations, notably Sheryl L. Pipe, Robin Fostel, and other staff at the ASPCA; Michelle Foncannon, Michelle Riley, and other staff of The Humane Society of the United States (HSUS); Stephanie Joos, Susan Northrup, and Terry Flick at Champaign County Animal Control; Annemarie Lucas; Adam Gankiewicz; and Mary "Tief" Tiefenbrunn and everyone else at the Champaign County Humane Society, Urbana, Illinois. I would also like to thank my editor and fellow dog lover, Erica Zappy, for her enthusiastic support and many contributions to *Rescuing Rover*.

As always, I would like to thank my wife, Linda, and our children, who have joined me in opening our hearts and sharing our home to so many beloved dogs, cats, and other pets over all these years.

Contents

Introduction 9

Pet Tragedy 15

Animal Welfare Organizations 37

Life in a Shelter 51

More About the ASPCA 70

Sources and Suggested Reading 72

About the Author and His Family Dogs 78

Index 80

INTRODUCTION

One sultry evening during the midst of a late summer heat wave, a young couple took their trash out to the Dumpster in the parking lot of their apartment complex. As the husband lifted the heavy metal lid, he noticed a pet carrier among the plastic bags of garbage.

Wondering why someone would throw away a brand-new pet carrier, he retrieved it, only to exclaim, "There's a puppy inside!"

The couple was shocked.

Someone had shoved a small black and white terrier inside the pet carrier, taped its mouth shut, and thrown it into the trash. No one knew how long the puppy had been trapped in the dark and suffocating heat of the Dumpster—one day, two days, or more—with no food or water. With the duct tape wrapped around its mouth, the dog couldn't bark or even pant. Hot, thirsty, and starving, she must have been terrified. Miraculously, she was alive . . . but just barely.

The couple called the local animal control department, and an officer soon arrived. As the officer carefully removed the puppy from the carrier, everyone wondered who would throw a little dog inside a Dumpster to suffer a slow death.

The animal control officer usually took abandoned, mistreated, and lost dogs to the shelter at the local humane society. However, she felt so sorry for this weak puppy that she took her home. The puppy was listless; she just lay there in shock. But the next day she drank a little water and nibbled some dog food, and she perked up.

Linda holds Suzie in our backyard on the very first day that she arrived in her new home. It was early October, just a month after Suzie had been found in a Dumpster.

Suzie has since made herself at home. She likes to run around the yard, ride in the car, bark at animals on television, and take little naps in the evenings.

About four months old, the puppy soon became bright-eyed and energetic, wagging her stubby tail as she scampered around the house. She loved to eat, play, and sleep, and occasionally she tinkled on the floor. She appeared to be a happy dog and a scrappy girl. But no one ever found out who had once owned the little spitfire and why she had been mistreated.

The veterinarian guessed that the dog was either a rat terrier or miniature fox terrier, all of fourteen pounds. But the *miniature* part never fooled anyone, especially the puppy who thought of herself as a big dog. As Mark Twain once quipped, "What counts is not necessarily the size of the dog in the fight, what counts is the size of the fight in the dog." And Suzie had plenty of fight in her. After all, she had survived a long ordeal in a hot metal box.

The animal control officer placed her in a foster home until she could be adopted. This home had rottweilers and Dobermans, which are tough dogs, but Suzie went easy on them and ended up pretty much running the place.

Like thousands of other rescued dogs, Suzie was featured on Petfinder.com, which is where my wife, Linda, and I noticed her photo and read her story. We already had two other rescued dogs and Leo, a Siamese cat, but there was room for more. We have been delighted to provide Suzie with a permanent home, known as a "forever home," for the rest of her life with our family. Our little dog now has the run of the house with Lucky, a Jack Russell terrier; Zander, a beagle/Lab mutt; Boone, a goofy Lab; and Leo and Isabel, our Siamese cats. Boone and Isabel came from our local humane society, where many of the photographs for this book were taken.

Millions of dogs, both mutts and purebreds, are rescued every year, and each of these dogs has a story. Many of these stories are not as dramatic as being thrown into the garbage, but other dogs have been treated worse than our spunky terrier. For thousands of years, dogs have been devoted work partners, beloved companions, and the favorite pets of

Humane officers step in when puppies and dogs are mistreated. Officer Adam Gankiewicz, who starred on *Animal Precinct*, holds a dog that was rescued by the American Society for the Prevention of Cruelty to Animals (ASPCA).

Opposite: Every year millions of pets are rescued from neglectful situations, such as this old dog kept behind a wire fence in an abandoned lot, with no food, water, or shelter.

humans. Yet ironically, because of overpopulation, neglect, and mistreatment, a tragic fate befalls millions of puppies and dogs every year.

Many dogs eventually find homes. Every year, however, some four million dogs in the United States have to be "put down"—or "put to sleep"—which has become a tragedy in our midst. I am hopeful that *Rescuing Rover* will help us to save more of our beloved animals and to become more responsible caretakers of the dogs, cats, and other pets that have placed their faith in us.

An ASPCA worker holds a beagle puppy that has been rescued and placed in a shelter. The puppy will receive good care until it is adopted into a loving home.

PET TRAGEDY

Who doesn't love a puppy? Who can ever not love a dog? According to the American Pet Products Association (APPA), Americans now own 77.5 million dogs. Thirty-nine percent of households have at least one dog, and many have two or more bright-eyed, tail-wagging dogs at home. Many people would agree with naturalist and author Gerald Durrell that a "house is not a home until it has a dog." And dogs love people.

Dogs, who are probably the descendants of the gray wolf, have a long shared history with humans, stretching back ages. There is clear evidence that dogs became genetically different from their wolf ancestors at least 15,000 years ago. Some scientists believe that the first bond between people and wolves may have occurred as early as 40,000 years ago—or even as long as 100,000 to 140,000 years ago.

It is not certain whether people approached the wolves, or if curious canines ventured up to the campfires of early hunters and gatherers. Like people, wolves are social animals. They live in packs, which are similar to human families. As wolves evolved into domesticated dogs, they accepted people as their leaders.

From the beginning, both people and dogs benefited from their new relationship. Working together, humans and dogs became better hunters. Dogs could track game with their sense of smell. Standing upright, people had a high vantage point and color vision to more easily spot prey—and enemies. Humans also had tools, which helped in hunting and preparing food. People made sure their dogs were fed and protected. Dogs were also trained to watch over flocks of sheep and goats and to warn people of approaching enemies. It seemed natural that humans and dogs would become companions.

Dogs spread throughout the world until they were soon everywhere. Siberian people crossed the Bering Strait with their dogs. This migration of Native Americans may not have survived without the help of sled dogs. Many Native American tribes relied on dogs as pack animals for generations, even after horses came to North America.

In Europe during the Middle Ages, wealthy people began to keep dogs as status symbols, and the number of dog breeds increased enormously. Dogs were bred for size, color, appearance, and temperament. There are now more than four hundred dog breeds, all descended from the wolf—even the smallest Chihuahua.

Dogs have worked and lived with people for so long that they are known as "man's best friend," an expression that is common in many languages. Dogs have many jobs: herding livestock, hunting (especially pointers, retrievers, and hounds), rodent control, guarding, pulling sleds, and even helping fishermen with nets. Today we have service dogs such as guide dogs, assistance dogs, hearing dogs, and even therapy dogs that help people who have physical or mental disabilities.

Opposite: A group of sportsmen gather with their hounds in preparation for a hunt. Over the years, different breeds of dogs were developed for many tasks, especially hunting and herding.

Some owners like to enter their dogs in shows for best of breed and for sports, including dogsledding and agility competitions. Most of us have bonded with dogs of all sizes and shapes as pets, and people have also become the dog's best friend.

Today, Americans spend billions of dollars every year on food, treats, toys, and state-of-the-art veterinary care for their canine companions. One would think that all dogs enjoyed wonderful lives in people's homes, but thousands of unwanted puppies are born every day. Millions of unwanted puppies and dogs have no home or lose their homes every year. According to the Humane Society of the United States (HSUS), animal shelters take in and care for six to eight million unwanted dogs and cats every year. Between three and four million of these animals ultimately have to be euthanized—or put to sleep—because homes cannot be found for them.

People and organizations have been working hard to encourage people to take better care of their pets and to adopt homeless dogs. Seventy-five percent of dogs in the United States are now spayed or neutered, and it is hoped that this number will continue to grow. Moreover, 19 percent of the dogs in American homes have been adopted from animal shelters. Every year, as many as three to four million shelter and rescue dogs in the United States find homes.

Animal shelters and rescue groups have begun to emphasize "no-kill" policies—or have attempted to do so. Many private animal welfare groups have also established no-kill shelters and rescue facilities across the United States. Except for medical reasons or serious temperament issues, these shelters do not euthanize dogs or other animals in their care. However, relying on meager public funding and private donations, these groups often struggle to provide care for the exploding numbers of dogs and other pets that are overwhelming their facilities. They also must work with dogs that are difficult to place: unadoptable dogs that are too old, aggressive, or suffering from chronic health problems.

Many dog breeds, such as pit bulls, can be difficult to place. However, Butch was lucky to find a couple who realized that he was a sweet and friendly dog.

Opposite: Dogs have a long shared history with humans, with many breeds developed in the Middle Ages. Dogs became a familiar sight on the streets of European and early American cities.

There are simply not enough homes for so many homeless dogs. Picked up as strays, given up by their owners, or seized from cruel situations, these dogs are placed in shelters for a few days to several months—until they are adopted or put to sleep. How can there be millions of unwanted dogs in America? Where did all the dogs come from?

Backyard Breeders and Puppy Mills

In what has become a cruel industry, irresponsible breeders, ranging from backyard breeders to puppy mills, have caused the overpopulation of unwanted dogs. Backyard breeders often have a pair of dogs and sell their litters through newspaper ads. Professional breeders sell puppies that are not show quality, meaning they don't meet the ideal breed specifications. Many are responsible breeders who try to place their puppies in good homes. But there are already too many dogs in the United States, and every year even more puppies are born, many of which end up abandoned, neglected, or mistreated.

Puppies sold in pet stores are usually cute and adorable, but these young dogs come from facilities that have come to be known as puppy mills. Puppy mills operate as breeding factories, where profit matters more than the care of the dogs.

An ASPCA worker rescues a small dog from a cage during a raid on a puppy mill in rural Tennessee. At this puppy mill, breeding dogs were kept in cages in dark rooms for their entire lives.

This puppy mill dog had probably never been on grass outside.

Unlike more responsible breeders, who strive to match healthy puppies with good families, owners of the "mills" treat puppies as products. Wholesalers buy puppies as young as eight weeks of age and market them to pet shops, which put them up for sale in cages or store windows—at steeply marked-up prices.

Puppy mills keep breeding dogs in overcrowded, shabby, and unsanitary cages—often rows of cages stacked on top of each other. To make waste cleanup easier, the cages have wire floors that injure paws and legs. Breeder dogs at mills often spend their entire lives in these cages, exposed to the weather or crammed inside filthy shacks where they never get the chance to feel the sun or take a single breath of fresh air.

After his first owner made an impulsive purchase at a pet store, former puppy mill dog Freddie ended up at a rescue league. Luckily, he was adopted and found a forever home, where he has been happy and healthy.

Imprisoned in these small cages, puppies and dogs seldom, if ever, have veterinary care, good food, or exercise. They don't get a chance to run around on grass or romp around a house playing with toys. Kept isolated in the small cages, these dogs never socialize with people. They are never touched, let alone petted or brushed, and therefore many become fearful or aggressive.

To maximize profits, dogs are bred again as soon as each litter is weaned, or separated, from its mother. Unable to recover between litters, the mother dogs become so exhausted that within a few years they can no longer have puppies. These dogs are almost always euthanized if they are not rescued by an organization. The mother and father of the puppy you see in the pet store window rarely ever make it out of the mill alive.

ASPCA veterinarians and staff inspect a small Boston terrier that was rescued from a puppy mill in rural Tennessee. Many of these dogs suffer from injuries and illnesses.

Raised in dirty cages, puppies are cleaned up when sold, and they may look perfect in pet stores—and in their new homes. However, many have fleas and ticks and develop such illnesses as distemper, kennel cough, intestinal parasites, and heartworm. Because of inferior breeding, the puppies may be prone to heart disease, hip dysplasia, diabetes, respiratory disorders, and other maladies. Treatment can be costly and very sad for a sick puppy and its new family.

Above: A puppy longs to be free of its filthy cage, where it has spent its entire life.

Opposite: In puppy mills, dogs are kept in cages stacked high. The cages are rarely cleaned and the dogs often do not have food or water.

Puppy mills first became a major enterprise after World War II, when the United States Department of Agriculture encouraged farmers to raise purebred puppies for profit. Breeding dogs did not require the hard work or the risk entailed in growing field crops and raising livestock. So old chicken coops and rabbit hutches were turned into cages and kennels for dogs. Like old industrial mills, these operations cranked out puppies as though they were assembly-line products. Both large and small pet stores quickly boomed with the thousands of puppies from this new industry.

In the 1970s, wholesalers, or middlemen, sought more puppy suppliers on the East Coast, so they convinced Amish farmers in eastern Pennsylvania to set up their own puppy mills. Over the next thirty years Lancaster County came to have more puppy mills than any county in the nation. This traditional Amish country acquired the unfortunate nickname of Puppy Mill Capital of the East. Today there are puppy mills across the nation, and Missouri now has more than any other state.

How can we put an end to puppy mills? People can take an active role in fighting them by working with such animal welfare groups as the ASPCA and The HSUS to pass laws that ensure that all animals bred to be pets are raised in healthy conditions. You can join the ASPCA Advocacy Brigade to keep up to date about current legislation to ban puppy mills.

Most important, do not buy a puppy from a pet store—or even shop at stores that sell puppies and dogs. That puppy probably came from a substandard puppy mill where dogs are routinely mistreated. And do not buy a puppy or any other product from a website that sells pets online either. Anyone can put up an appealing website claiming high standards of breeding and care, but one really has no way of knowing if such businesses are legitimate. Truly responsible breeders want to meet buyers in person so they may be assured that each and every one of their pups goes to a good home.

Opposite: Abbie had a long journey from breeder to family to animal shelter, until she finally got lucky and found a permanent home.

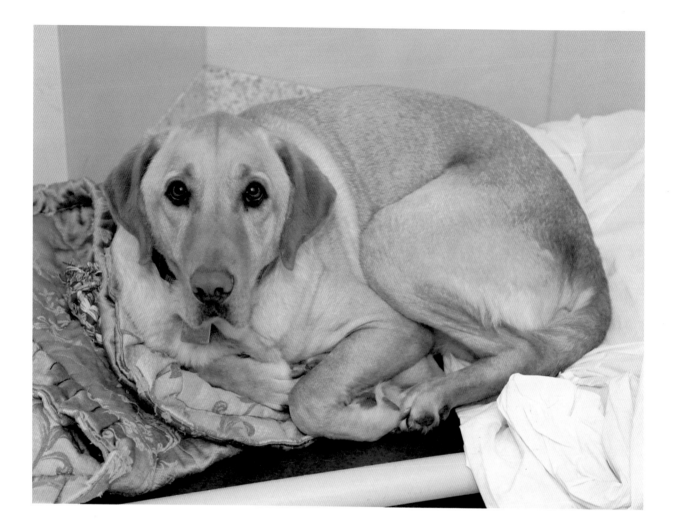

Even sweet dogs, like this mutt at the ASPCA shelter, may be difficult to place in homes because they are old and may need special care owing to health or age.

If you're looking for a puppy or dog to become part of your family, think about adopting from a shelter or a rescue organization. Not only will you be saving a life, you will not be supporting a puppy mill. There are many dogs waiting for homes in shelters all across the country—and about one in four is a purebred that probably came from a mill or other irresponsible breeder. If you still can't find the perfect dog, or if you have your heart set on a specific breed that you can't find in a shelter, you can do an Internet search for a nearby shelter or dog rescue for that breed. If more people adopted dogs from shelters and rescues, most of the unwanted puppies and dogs would finally have homes.

This man found a mother dog and her puppies abandoned on the side of a road. He brought them to the local shelter, where they would receive care and be adopted out to good homes.

Pet Owners

Many pet owners contribute to the overpopulation of dogs—some with the best of intentions and others thoughtlessly. People often happily acquire a dog on impulse. They become excited about having a cuddly puppy as a gift for a birthday, Christmas, or other occasion. However, the new owners soon realize that caring for the pet involves a lot of work and more expense than they had anticipated, and they become reluctant, unwilling, or unable to accept these responsibilities.

Some owners experience life changes, such as losing a job or moving to a new apartment where pets are not allowed. Occasionally, children or adults develop allergies to their dogs and must give them up. Or sadly, the owner dies, and no one in the family wants to keep the pet or is able to do so. A dog may also develop health problems that make it impossible for the owner to keep him because of the time and expense of veterinary care.

Other people simply do not take proper care of their dogs. These owners don't even provide the basics of food, water, and shelter. Many never take their dogs to the veterinarian for shots or other medical care. Thousands suffer and die each year because irresponsible people no longer bother with their care. Others are trained to engage in vicious criminal activities, such as dogfighting, and some dogs are beaten by their owners. These people do not reflect upon their own cruelties. Many of these owners also do not neuter or spay their dogs, which then run loose and breed with other dogs. As a result, there are thousands of mixed litters every year that contribute to the millions of unwanted pets in the United States.

Some owners simply leave an unwanted puppy on a city street or dump an old dog in a ditch along a country road. Unable to fend for themselves, if they are not found and rescued, these abandoned animals invariably die of hunger, freeze to death, or get hit by a car. More responsible owners take an unwanted dog to an animal shelter or contact a rescue group,

Opposite: A HSUS staff member cradles a small terrier in her arms. Rescued from a bad situation, the dog will receive medical care before being adopted into a new, safe home.

where the pet will be cared for until it can, with luck, be placed in a new home.

However, whether public or private, these organizations are all critically underfunded. Lacking staff and space, many shelters, especially those in large cities, are so overwhelmed with dogs and cats that they cannot find homes for every animal in their care. Moreover, some dogs are very hard to place because of age, health, or behavioral problems. Certain dogs may have been bred to fight, and others that may be aggressive and not well socialized are often unsuitable for adoption. Unless quickly adopted, these pets often have to be humanely euthanized.

The HSUS engages in many activities, including the rescue of dogs from puppy mills and from dogfighting, saving pets in hurricanes, and encouraging adoption from local shelters.

Opposite: A humane officer removed this pit bull puppy from an abusive home and placed her in a shelter. Dog behaviorists were able to socialize the young dog, who was adopted by a kind family.

THE AMERICAN SOCIETY FOR THE PREVENTION OF CRUELTY TO ANIMALS

OFFICE

SHELTER

As shown in this early photograph of a woman, a young man, and two dogs in front of the New York City headquarters, the ASPCA has been protecting dogs since its founding.

ANIMAL WELFARE ORGANIZATIONS

Over the years, several kinds of animal welfare organizations have emerged in the United States, notably the ASPCA, The HSUS, and thousands of local shelters, animal sanctuaries, rescues, and, in recent years, websites. From small towns and rural counties to bustling cities, from Boston to San Francisco and from the Florida Keys to Juneau, Alaska, these organizations and the people who work for them have devoted themselves to rescuing puppies, dogs, and other household pets every day of the year.

The ASPCA

Founded by Henry Bergh in 1866, the American Society for the Prevention of Cruelty to Animals was the first humane society established in North America. Incorporated that year by a special act of the New York State Legislature, the ASPCA's mission, as stated by Bergh, was "to provide effective means for the prevention of cruelty to animals throughout the United States." Over the years, the ASPCA has faced many challenges and enjoyed many triumphs—ensuring protection and care for New York City's working horses, transforming dog pounds into professionally run adoptions centers, and establishing an animal hospital in New York City that is still operating today.

The ASPCA is one of the most effective animal welfare organizations in the world. With more than one million supporters, it maintains successful anticruelty programs throughout the United States and is recognized nationally. It was also the first humane organization to be granted legal authority to investigate and make arrests for crimes against animals.

Today the ASPCA maintains a state-of-the-art animal shelter at its national headquarters in Manhattan and encourages adoption of dogs in local shelters across the country. The organization suggests, "If you can't decide between a Shepherd, a Setter or a Poodle, get them all . . . adopt a mutt!"

The ASPCA adoption van has become a familiar sight on the streets of New York City. The van has been helpful in promoting the adoption of cats, dogs, and other pets, not only in Manhattan but also throughout the United States.

The Humane Society of the United States

The largest animal protection organization in the nation, The Humane Society of the United States has eleven million members—one in every twenty-eight people in the country. Established in 1954 in Washington, D.C., The HSUS became a new kind of organization, based in the nation's capital, to confront the root causes of animal cruelty throughout the country. From its founding, The HSUS has sought "a humane and sustainable world for all animals—a world that will also benefit people."

The HSUS provides care for thousands of animals at its sanctuaries and rescue facilities, wildlife rehabilitation centers, and mobile veterinary clinics. It further serves as a relief agency for animals during national disasters. Every year the organization launches new programs, such as Humane Wildlife Services, to provide homeowners and businesses with humane and effective ways to resolve conflicts with wildlife.

The HSUS confronts animal cruelty through national and international campaigns against the blood sports of dogfighting and cockfighting, against puppy mills where dogs are treated like factory machines, and against the worst animal cruelties of modern agribusiness. It also takes other actions to protect wild and domestic animals. The Humane Society of the United States is a powerful advocate for animals, lobbying for the passage of many laws in the U.S. Congress and state legislatures and promoting animal welfare and humane treatment in courtrooms and corporate boardrooms. They are the nation's most important advocate for local humane societies, providing shelter standards and evaluations, training programs, a national advertising campaign to promote pet adoption, and national conferences. The HSUS publishes *All Animals,* a membership magazine, and *Animal Sheltering,* a bimonthly magazine for animal shelter professionals.

Above and opposite:
In animal shelters across
the United States, thousands
of puppies and dogs wait
to find permanent homes.
Anyone who has adopted a
shelter dog like these two,
knows they make wonderful
and grateful pets.

Public Animal Shelters

Public shelters house lost, abandoned, and unwanted animals, primarily dogs and cats. The animals are kept at shelters until reclaimed by their owners, adopted by a new owner, placed with another organization—or put to sleep. These public facilities are usually funded and operated by local governments or run on behalf of cities or counties. Many of the people who work at these shelters generously volunteer their help.

The agencies often enforce local pet laws too, and provide services related to domestic and, sometimes, wild animals. They also provide veterinary care, including examinations, vaccinations, spaying, and neutering. Many shelters also offer animal behavior training and education services for pet owners and adopters.

Animal shelters were once known as "dog pounds," a term that came from *pounds* in small villages, where stray cattle, sheep, and other livestock were once penned up until claimed by their owners. Referring to an "enclosed place for animals," the word *pound* comes from late Old English *pund-fald*, which became *penfold* and then *pound*. The Glocester Town Pound is believed to be the oldest dog pound in America still in existence. Built in 1748 to confine stray farm animals, this stone enclosure came to be used for dogs as well. Added to the National Register of Historic Places in 1970, it is now a historic site on Pound Road and Chopmist Hill Road in Glocester, Rhode Island.

Private Shelters

Not-for-profit groups often operate their own private shelters supported by donations from individuals and businesses. There are thousands of these shelters in the United States, ranging in size from modest storefronts to entire buildings. Shelters usually work in cooperation with and assistance from local city and county governments in caring for dogs and other domestic animals. Many are "open-door shelters" that accept all dogs and other pets that come through their doors. They do not charge a fee, although they will gladly accept donations. Most shelters either have or are striving toward a no-kill policy, which means that no healthy animal will ever be put to sleep.

Animal Sanctuaries

At Best Friends Animal Sanctuary, hundreds of animals, including dogs (like Garret, above), cats, pigs, horses, and birds wait for their forever homes. If they are not adopted, they will live out their years at the sanctuary.

Animal sanctuaries will accept and care for animals for the rest of their natural lives, often without trying to find any other home for them. Many sanctuaries take in animals that are not adoptable, such as feral cats and dogs, wild animals, abused pets requiring special care, farm animals, and pets with medical or behavioral problems. Animal sanctuaries strive to provide an ideal life for dogs, especially for older and special-needs animals that cannot find homes. However, animal sanctuaries are quite expensive to operate and can care for only a small number of needy animals. One of the most effective sanctuaries is the Best Friends Animal Sanctuary at Angel Canyon, not too far from the Grand Canyon and Bryce Canyon in Kanab, Utah. This well-known sanctuary can house some two thousand dogs, cats, farm animals, birds, and small animals at any time. They come from shelters and rescue groups across the United States.

Profile of an Animal Shelter

"The Champaign County Humane Society was established as a branch of the Illinois Humane Society in 1889 and chartered in 1903. Those early years were focused on the protection of animals and children. In 1951 a diverse group of local citizens who cared deeply about animals gathered together to establish our first animal shelter, near Bondville, Illinois, and in June 1988 we moved into our current shelter in Urbana.

"Our name reflects our geographic location only. We are not a government body, and we are not supported by tax dollars. We are not affiliated with any national organization. We are an 'open-door' shelter and accept all animals needing shelter, regardless of age, physical condition, or adoptability. As a local, not-for-profit charity, we exist through the generosity of many individuals and businesses and are supported by a community that cares."

—Champaign County Humane Society website

Champaign County Humane Society is an open-door shelter that accepts and cares for dogs, cats, and other unwanted pets. It provides food and shelter along with medical care and training.

An early ASPCA animal enforcement officer receives a lick from a grateful German shepherd. The ASPCA has long had police authority in protecting animals from abuse and neglect.

Protecting Our Pets: Humane Officers

Anyone who has lost a dog can thank the local humane officer for help in finding the pet. These dedicated men and women work for a city or county, and they respond to calls for help in finding stray animals or investigating reports of cruelty to dogs and other animals. Sometimes called animal care officers, animal control officers, animal cops, or even the puppy police, these individuals bring lost, injured, and abandoned dogs to local shelters, where they are held until claimed by their owners, put up for adoption, or sometimes put to sleep.

Humane officers are also responsible for investigating dog bites. They often work with police and other city officials in resolving any problems with dogs. Over the past several decades, the position has changed from that of a simple dog-catcher to a devoted, knowledgeable, and compassionate public servant. Humane officers now emphasize pet care education and help to rescue animals from dangerous or cruel situations. And sometimes they care for injured wildlife.

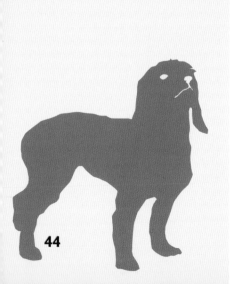

ASPCA humane officer Annemarie Lucas became one of the stars and heroines on *Animal Precinct*. This popular television program brought national attention to the plight of many puppies and dogs in the United States.

Humane control officers typically work for a local government, often as members of the police department, or they may be contracted by the local private shelter. Depending on the size of the city and county and the level of funding, a community may have just one animal control officer or a departmental team.

More than 150 years ago Abraham Lincoln declared, "I am in favor of animal rights as well as human rights. That is

Most rescue groups specialize in different animals or various breeds — not just dogs, but birds, turtles, ferrets, and other species. Some work to find good homes for cats, such as this kitten above. Others rescue farm animals that have been neglected, such as this starving horse, opposite.

the way of a whole human being." Increasingly, people have come to recognize these rights and local governments have passed tougher animal protection laws—and have begun to enforce them. Armed and trained as police, many animal control officers are now involved in criminal investigations of animal cruelty.

For many years the New York branch of the ASPCA employed several "animal cops" who carried firearms and had police authority. This practice has become more common throughout the United States, especially in urban areas where animal control officers face difficult investigations. The animal cops have devoted themselves to the protection and rescue of any animal in need.

Other Animal Rescue Organizations

Established and managed by volunteers, not-for-profit animal rescue groups share the same goals as public and private shelters—taking in abandoned or stray pets and finding good new homes for them. However, instead of a kennel or other physical location for sheltering dogs, rescue groups often rely on foster homes. Members or friends of these rescue groups temporarily take animals into their own homes. These dog lovers provide not only food and shelter but also veterinary care and training, until a good permanent home can be found. Rescue groups scrape by on private donations and adoption fees to support their efforts. Like animal shelters, they can barely cover the significant costs of rescuing and caring for unwanted pets.

Most rescue groups work with one species of animal, not only dogs or cats, but also rabbits, birds, farm animals, and other species. Rescue groups for dogs sometimes specialize in types of dogs, such as hunting dogs, large dogs, and so forth, or they work with specific breeds, such as Labrador retrievers, poodles, and many others. These groups often work in cooperation with a national club for the dog breed.

Virtually all rescue groups are committed to a no-kill policy. They often work closely with local shelters that are overwhelmed with dogs and cats. When the shelters become overcrowded, rescue groups scramble to find more volunteers to provide foster homes for dogs that would otherwise be put to sleep. For example, when Echo Dogs White Shepherd Rescue finds an unwanted white German shepherd, this group of volunteers finds a foster home for the dog, cares for it, and then places it in a suitable home.

Rescue groups can succeed only when people are willing to provide forever homes for cats, dogs, and other unwanted animals. To make sure that animals are placed in good homes, rescue groups have strict adoption requirements that include a completed application, veterinary reference, telephone interview, and home visit.

Foster Homes

Some of the dogs that find their way into shelters and rescues aren't ready to be adopted, because they are sick, frightened, unfriendly, or pregnant. Many puppies are too young to survive in a shelter or have never known a kind person. Stray dogs are often placed in foster homes so that more can be learned about their temperament. To give these special-needs puppies and dogs the best chance of finding a permanent home, they are often placed in foster homes until they're ready to be adopted.

Becoming a foster parent affords someone an opportunity to help animals that would otherwise never have a chance. A foster parent might care for a stray mother and her litter of puppies until she rebuilds her strength and her babies are old enough to be weaned and adopted. A foster parent might take in a dog undergoing heartworm treatment, or a frightened mutt that simply needs a patient and loving family. Or a foster parent might help a young puppy mill dog that has never been inside a home and never learned how to play.

Some dogs require little care from their foster parents. A healthy puppy may need to be in a home for only a week or two until it is old enough to be adopted. The foster parent will provide food and water, begin to housetrain the puppy, and play with it. Other dogs require a major commitment. A litter of orphaned puppies must be bottle-fed every few hours, or an old dog may have to be given medication twice a day.

Foster families sometimes work only with puppies, while others are behavioral experts who work with dogs that are timid or aggressive and need to be socialized. Other foster families will take any dog in need, no matter what the situation. Foster parents need to consider just how much responsibility they are prepared to accept for their puppies and dogs, and they must also consider other family members—spouses, children, and other pets—to minimize any stress.

Fostering can be a wonderful way for children to learn about dogs and the daily responsibilities of caring for a pet. But it can also be difficult, even heartbreaking, if a foster dog is sick and doesn't survive. At times a foster family may become so attached to a dog they don't want to let it go.

Many shelters offer volunteer orientation and training programs for people who wish to become foster parents for dogs and other pets. A staff veterinarian will interview the prospective foster parents and provide them with literature about this very important work. In many states, foster parents must also apply for a license and pay a small annual fee. Sometimes the shelter or rescue will provide food, medicine, and supplies, but foster parents often contribute financially as well as donate their time to caring for their beloved puppies and dogs.

Shelter staff and rescue volunteers work closely with new foster parents. Usually people start off slowly by bringing home a frightened and lonely dog that just needs love and attention, or a couple of puppies to look after for a week or two—before dealing with more challenging dogs. As foster parents gain experience, they can help mentor new foster parents. Shelter staff members, including veterinarians, are often available to help with any questions or concerns.

Over the years, foster programs across the United States have become well organized and quite effective in saving the lives of puppies and dogs, and foster parents are among the most dedicated and loving of people who help in rescue efforts.

Many surrendered dogs in overcrowded shelters and rescue groups find their way into foster care until they are placed in permanent homes. Wally came into a shelter over the Thanksgiving holiday, so he spent the week with a shelter volunteer before he was adopted.

A young dog waiting to be adopted at the Champaign County Humane Society in Illinois.

LIFE IN A SHELTER

"An animal's eyes have the power
to speak a great language."
—*Martin Buber*

There are thousands of public and private shelters across the United States, all of which are committed to the rescue and care of dogs, cats, and other pets. Most shelters manage to help millions of unwanted pets despite tight budgets, crowded kennels, and small staffs, including hard-working volunteers. No one can predict how each day will unfold at the shelter—except that employees will be very busy. "Every day I wake up wondering what the day will bring," says Ellen LeKostaj, animal caretaker and adoption counselor at Tails Humane Society in DeKalb, Illinois. "It could be full of joy and happiness or it could be tear-filled and heart-wrenching. More often than not, it's a little of both."

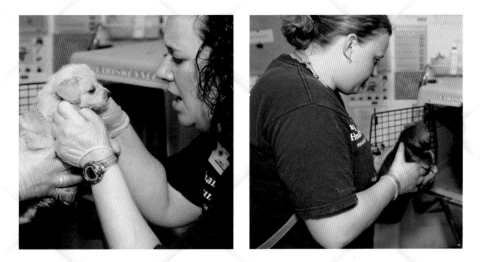

Vet techs look over puppies that have just been dropped off at a shelter. Skilled techs carefully examine every animal that comes in.

On any given day, the animal control officer may drop off a starving dog—and her litter of puppies—that had been tied to a Dumpster. Someone may surrender an old dog he doesn't want anymore, or another person may carry in a young cat that's been hit by a car. Adoption counselors gather as much information as possible for each pet taken into the shelter. Veterinarians and technicians then examine the puppy or dog and treat any illnesses or injuries. Trained staff will vaccinate

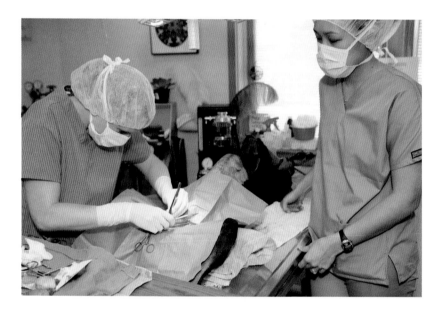

Two veterinarians operate on an older dog, which will soon be ready for adoption. All the dogs at the shelter are spayed or neutered so that they will not have any unwanted puppies.

Veterinarians follow up on all the medical care of every puppy and dog, such as these two dogs who wear cone collars, also known as Elizabethan collars or E-collars, after surgery.

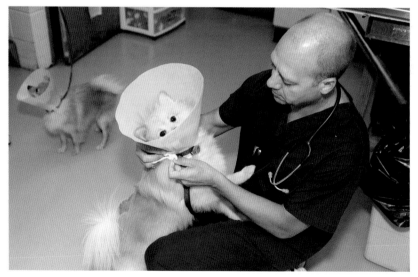

puppies and dogs. Often they will schedule adult male canines to be neutered or females to be spayed, meaning they won't be able to have more puppies.

Puppies are placed in cages, and dogs are put into kennels with clean, comfortable bedding (towels and blankets), along with food and fresh water. Staff and volunteers follow a busy routine in caring for the many animals housed at the shelter—cleaning kennels, feeding, watering, and walking daily.

Animal shelters need piles of old newspapers to use in cages for puppies and cats, as well as donated blankets and towels, which may be used for bedding in the many crates and kennels they use.

Animal shelters need bags of dog food piled high and rows of canned food to satisfy all the hungry puppies and dogs. Feeding so many animals every day quickly becomes very expensive. Here, a volunteer prepares a peanut butter treat for one of the dogs.

Opposite: Among the most important and enjoyable jobs for both volunteers and dogs are daily walks.

In both public and private shelters, knowledgeable, dedicated professional employees and volunteers feed and water all the animals every day. They clean cages and kennels and wash and dry mountains of bedding in the laundry. Others, often volunteers, take the dogs on daily walks in the fields around the shelter and assist those who would like to adopt a new pet.

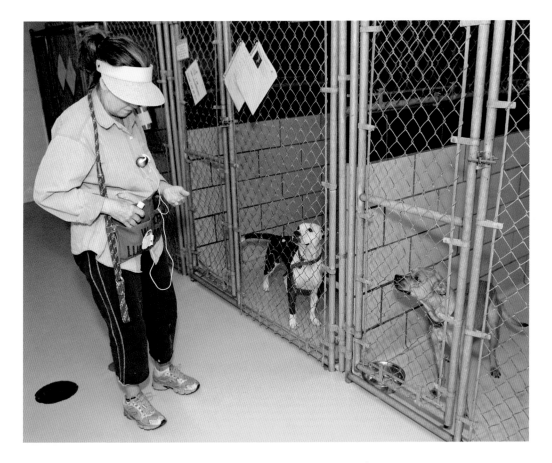

Lots of dogs mean a lot of walks every day, so shelters need a good supply of leashes. Dog leashes of various sizes and styles line the walls at this local shelter.

Shelters often place information, including photographs of adoptable dogs, on their websites and link with Internet sites such as Petfinder.com. People can then look at adoptable dogs before visiting the shelter.

Pet Adoption

Pet adoption is one of the best ways to solve the animal over-population crisis—and save the life of an innocent dog. Animal welfare advocates urge people to adopt dogs from shelters, rescues, or previous owners instead of buying pure-bred puppies from pet stores or breeders. Through pet adoption, an individual or a family can take responsibility for a dog that has been abandoned, neglected, or mistreated. The new owners become lifetime guardians who love and care for the rescued dogs, which make loving pets. Adoption greatly reduces the number of dogs who have to be put to sleep every year.

People can find unwanted dogs through newspaper advertisements placed by owners who are no longer able to care for their dogs and must find new homes for their pets. They can also visit local animal shelters to look for dogs, as well as cats and other pets. Dogs adopted from shelters were once known as pound puppies, but today they are more commonly called shelter

dogs. People wanting to adopt a dog of a certain breed can also contact one of the many rescue groups that have been established in recent years. Dogs adopted from these organizations are often referred to as rescue dogs (not to be confused with search and rescue dogs!).

Over the past decade or so, online pet adoption through Internet sites has become an especially popular and effective way of finding homes for unwanted pets. Thousands of shelters and rescue groups across the United States have established their own websites featuring photos of adoptable pets to help people choose the right dog or cat for their family. These websites are often linked with Internet sites, such as Petfinder.com, that maintain databases of pets available from animal shelters and rescue groups. Information about hundreds of thousands of dogs, including photographs, is featured on these websites. Online pet adoption through Internet sites can be an excellent way of matching families and dogs.

People who volunteer at or make donations to their local shelter often like to wear a T-shirt or display stickers that show their support for the organization and its hard-working staff.

Children and elementary school classes who visit the animal shelter contribute art-work and stories to brighten the walls at Champaign County Humane Society.

A Day in the Life of an Animal Shelter Worker

Many shelter workers have had years of experience in helping puppies, dogs, and other pets. Here is a typical day in the life of Ellen LeKostaj, whose work is similar to that at shelters across the United States: "Every day there are cat cages to tidy, litter to scoop, dogs to walk, and kisses to dole out to all of the fuzzy and feathered. I'm generally a bit frazzled trying to get the public areas spotless and taken care of by the time we open. It's a race against the clock, and it seems like the clock always wins. The general chaos increases as the public pours in at noon, asking questions, petting, touching, adopting.

"Once the animals are fed and taken care of, it's time to feed the public with information about responsible pet ownership. I explain that some cats need to be coaxed to eat; some dogs will eat anything—edible or not. Some people don't want to hear a word I have to say regarding their dog's behavior problems. Others are starving for information, asking me to explain in detail the history of clicker

training and all of its applications. I try to reach out to them all, just as I try to reach out to each animal with a caress or a kind word. Some people remind me of the kind of dogs that you handle with a rabies pole. They make me cringe inside, but I still try to disarm them with thoughtful answers and a calm smile.

"The phone rings over and over. It's raining outside, but I didn't realize it was raining stray cats. We don't have space, but we make room for a litter of orphan kittens. We make room again for an injured cat. We're playing what I affectionately call 'cat Tetris.' It involves moving one cat, scrubbing its cage for another cat, scrubbing that cat's cage for yet another cat, combining two cats into one cage, scrubbing another cage and . . . voilà! . . . we have a cage for the injured cat.

People often want puppies, and this bright-eyed golden retriever will soon be adopted, as are most young dogs. However, it is often hard to place older dogs, who also need homes.

"Meanwhile, the evening rush comes in. I'm doing three adoptions at once. My coworkers are struggling to walk dogs among the throngs of people in our adoption area. It's dinnertime for the cats, and they're letting us know. I need health exams done on all three animals being adopted, the phone won't stop ringing, and I feel terrible for the volunteer trying to learn to do adoptions. Students for our obedience class are trickling in, and they want to share updates on their dogs' progress. My head is spinning already, and there's still so much to do tonight.

"It isn't until late, after evening walks are done, medications are given, obedience class ends, and the doors are locked, that the building falls silent. I turn off the classical music, and I can hear the rain on the roof. In the next room I hear the clicking of a rabbit's water bottle. The puppies snuggle in a heap. The cats are lounging in their cages. All is well for tonight. We'll start over tomorrow. For now, life is good."

Employees at a local shelter face long, hard, and occasionally sad days, but there are also many joys, such as holding a kitten that has just been rescued. This kitten will soon be adopted into a loving home.

Everyone loves a puppy, including the shelter workers and volunteers who care for all the animals. This shelter worker couldn't resist holding a puppy that had just arrived.

59

Animal Shelter Policies

- Shelters place animals only in *permanent, responsible* homes. Adopters are asked to carefully consider the time and expense of owning a pet as a lifetime commitment. Adopters must be twenty-one years of age or older.

- They must complete an adoption application at the facility, followed by a mandatory twenty-four-hour waiting period before a pet can go to a new home.

- All animals leaving the shelter must be spayed or neutered, in accordance with state law.

- Adopted pets must be taken to a veterinarian for a health exam within one week after leaving the shelter.

- Before adopting a pet anyone renting or leasing a house or apartment must provide the shelter with approval from the landlord.

- Most shelters will not place an animal with a person or family who is moving or planning to do so within a month after adoption.

- Animals may be adopted into homes as pets or companions only. Cats are not adopted as mousers on farms and dogs are not placed as strictly guard or protective animals.

- Shelters will not allow the adoption of puppies or dogs that will be kept outside.

- Shelters do not allow animals to be adopted as gifts or presents for others.

- Many shelters suggest or require that the owners provide a fenced-in yard, especially for large dogs (over forty pounds).

- Ideally, a dog should be walked every day on a leash.

- Most shelters do not recommend adopting puppies or kittens in a family with very young children or in a situation where all adults are gone for long periods each day.

- If, at any time, the adopter can no longer care for the pet, he or she is required to return the pet to the shelter or the closest humane society.

- The shelter reserves the right to refuse any adoption.

These policies are based on the Champaign County Humane Society's policies and are typical of those of local public shelters in the United States. Always check with an organization to make sure you know its policies.

How to Adopt a Dog

Animal shelters make great efforts to ensure that puppies and dogs are adopted into good homes. Many ask people to consider the following points before adopting a pet.

DO YOUR HOMEWORK

Before visiting a shelter, stop by the library or search the Internet for information about breeds of dogs, especially their needs regarding diet, exercise, medical care, and general behavior or temperament. There are so many breeds that deciding on a dog can be overwhelming. However, the wide variety in size and temperament can also help in selecting a type of dog that best matches the lifestyle of its owner. Someone who runs five miles may prefer an active dog for a companion. A less active person might want a buddy with whom to lounge around the house.

A family with children may be looking for a dog that will be tolerant and playful with kids. In fact, children should help in selecting the dog and visiting the shelter, otherwise they may be disappointed if the choice is not appropriate.

Anyone who rents an apartment or a house should first check whether there are restrictions on the type of pets and their size.

61

Most shelters do a complete assessment of all puppies and dogs and provide helpful information about health and temperament on the kennel door.

MAKING A CHOICE

Once you have a good idea of the kind of dog that you'd like, you can telephone the local shelter or look at adoptable pets on its website. You can then visit the shelter during regular adoption hours.

Allow between one and two hours, or longer, for a visit. Depending on the number of dogs you wish to get acquainted with, your previous experience with pet care, and the number of other visitors to the shelter, the process can take some time. Most shelters are especially busy on weekends, Friday afternoons, and Monday mornings.

On the door of each dog's cage is a card with basic information: breed, age, sex, neuter status, and a little history, along with its name and an identification number. A staff person can use this identification number to provide you with additional information about the dog.

Looking at puppies and dogs at the local shelter can be a great way to find a wonderful pet and a best friend.

This mother and her daughters are getting acquainted with a young dog in a special room at the shelter. They can also walk the dog and play with him in an outdoor kennel.

Shelter employees want to make sure that dogs go to good, permanent homes, so they call references listed on an adoption application.

GETTING ACQUAINTED

Once you have found a puppy or dog that you might want to adopt, a staff member or volunteer adoption counselor will let you visit in a "get-acquainted room," or you can take the dog outside for a walk or in a large kennel. It is important that everyone in the household gets to know and enjoy the animal before the adoption is completed.

If you already have other dogs, many shelters suggest that all the dogs get together for a visit under the guidance of a behavior expert to help insure that they get along and make a smooth transition into the home.

PAPERWORK

If you decide to adopt a dog, you will need to fill out an application, and a sticker is placed on the pet's cage card to notify others that an adoption is pending. Animals will usually not be "held" for anyone unless an adoption application has been completed.

An adoption counselor of the shelter will review the application with you and explain the level of care required by the dog. The counselor may ask additional questions about your home and lifestyle to make sure you and the dog will be a good fit for each other.

Once the counselor has discussed the application with you, the adoption will be either refused or tentatively approved. Final approval will be determined within a day or two, depending on the final physical exam of the dog and other factors, such as verification of landlord approval.

Shelters require adopters to complete an application to make sure that dogs go to good homes. Staff members are also happy to answer any questions about the adoption steps.

Sometimes it is hard not to fall in love with all of the pets at a shelter. Spending time with each one helps make the final decision easier.

THINKING IT OVER

While awaiting final approval, you will be given some useful literature about the responsibilities and joys of having a new pet. Adopting is a major decision—it can be a ten- to twenty-year commitment for the life of the dog. The mandatory twenty-four-hour waiting period also allows you time to prepare your home for the new dog and plan for your new arrival.

ASKING QUESTIONS

On the day of pickup, you should call the shelter to check on final approval of your application. The receptionist or adoption counselor will inform you of any health problems that have been identified and what kind of follow-up care will be needed. If you have doubts or questions regarding the health status of the pet, you will be encouraged to speak with the veterinary technician or veterinarian on staff, or to consult your own vet prior to finalizing the adoption.

This woman found a shelter dog that appeals to her. She is taking a quick photograph to show to her husband, and she hopes he will also like the dog and want to bring him home.

Scrappy Kristi was put up for adoption and soon found a new home and a loving owner, thanks to the animal rescue efforts and professional care of the ASPCA.

Like many strays and abandoned dogs, Suzy found her way into a shelter in New York City. Eventually she found a new home and a loving owner, thanks to the animal rescue efforts of the ASPCA.

GOING HOME!

When you arrive at the shelter to pick up your new dog, you will be given an adoption contract that must be signed. You will be asked to pay an adoption fee, so bring along cash, credit card, or checkbook—as well as a leash. This fee typically pays for vaccines, ID tag, and microchip, and helps with shelter costs.

Shelters want dogs to be adopted into permanent homes. So if you're not sure that you're prepared to care for a pet, you may withdraw an adoption application at any time during the process. Many shelters allow, or even require, people to return dogs if the adopters find that they cannot take care of them.

It is so exciting to bring home a new dog—for you and the dog. That puppy in the pet store window may have been cute, but adopted dogs somehow realize that they have been rescued, and they tend to be grateful and happy that you have given them a "second chance" in life.

Owning a pet is both a right and a responsibility. Through educational programs and legislation at the local, state, and national level, people can learn how to take good care of their pets, and through these positive actions and the good work of individuals and animal welfare organizations, the crisis facing dogs and other pets can ultimately be resolved. May all of us become like the dog lover who quipped, "My goal in life is to be as good of a person as my dog already thinks I am."

Boone, left, spent his entire life out-doors. Malnourished, he had never been to the vet, and was adopted with some special needs. Now he is a happy and healthy boy.

MORE ABOUT THE ASPCA

Among its wide-ranging activities, the ASPCA is especially committed to helping people care for their animal companions through a variety of services:

- The specially trained staff at the ASPCA Animal Poison Control Center is on call around the clock.

- The ASPCA Animal Behavior Center offers free expert training and behavior advice.

- The organization maintains the full-service, accredited Bergh Memorial Animal Hospital in New York City with a dedicated staff of veterinarians ready to provide high-quality medical care.

- A fleet of ASPCA mobile spay/neuter clinics serves low-income communities throughout New York City.

- Pet loss support services are offered for those who are grieving.

- The ASPCA has especially dedicated itself to helping the country's at-risk animals.

- The ASPCA Mission: Orange initiative fosters partnerships with key cities across the United States to end the unnecessary euthanasia of adoptable pets.

- ASPCA disaster readiness experts work with state agencies to create plans for animals in times of emergency.

- At its headquarters in New York City, the ASPCA operates an eight-thousand-square-foot state-of-the-art adoption facility.

- To help shelters find compatible homes for thousands of animals each year, the ASPCA has developed a research-based adoption program, ASPCA Meet Your Match.

- The organization also continues its work of helping at-risk horses with the ASPCA Equine Fund.

- The ASPCA has launched a bold and vigorous campaign combining its animal protection efforts with the newest technology for solving crimes of animal cruelty.

- The ASPCA Anti-Cruelty Center in New York City will be the very first of its kind in the world. Its Humane Law Enforcement department—which continues to uphold New York City's animal cruelty laws—will work with forensics experts to help investigate and prosecute crimes against animals.

- The ASPCA helps educate police officers, humane investigators, veterinarians, prosecutors, and judges on how to respond to animal cruelty, and it assists in cruelty case investigations.

- ASPCA animal advocates fight tirelessly on state and national levels to pass laws that protect animals.

SOURCES AND SUGGESTED READING

Here is a brief list of books that were consulted for *Rescuing Rover*, along with websites for the ASPCA, The HSUS, and other organizations devoted to the rescue and care of dogs. Surprisingly, to date, there are few nonfiction children's books about the broad national campaign of rescuing dogs, despite the significance of this crisis and the growing concern throughout the United States.

Books for Children

American Kennel Club. *Complete Dog Book for Kids*. New York: Howell Book House, 1996.

Casey, Patricia. *One Day at Wood Green Animal Shelter*. London: Walker, 2001.

Cheehy, Debra, and Carol Hilliard. *I Like Dogs*. Manassas, Va.: Four Foot Press, 2009.

Craig, Lynda, Sue Armstrong, and Sharon Wadsworth-Smith. *The Adventures of Gus and Us: Based on a True Story*. Caledon, Ontario: Canine Adventures, 2006.

Curtis, Patricia, and David Cupp. *The Animal Shelter*. New York: E. P. Dutton, 1984.

Dike, Diane, Craig A. Grasso, and Samantha A. Grasso. *Gracie Comes Home*. Lake City, Colo.: Western Reflections, 2007.

Furstinger, Nancy, Sheryl Pipe, and the American Society for the Prevention of Cruelty to Animals. *Kids Making a Difference for Animals*. Hoboken, N.J.: Wiley, 2009.

Gutman, Bill, and Anne Canevari Green. *Adopting Pets: How to Choose Your New Best Friend*. Brookfield, Conn.: Millbrook Press, 2001.

Houk, Randy. *Jasmine: A True Story from the Northeast Animal Shelter.* Fairfield, Conn.: Benefactory, 1993.

Howey, Paul, and Judy Mehn Zabriskie. *Freckles: The Mystery of the Little White Dog in the Desert: A True Story.* Phoenix: AZTexts, 2003.

Isler, Claudia. *Volunteering to Help Animals.* New York: Children's Press, 2000.

Jackson, Emma, and Bob Carey. *A Home for Dixie: The True Story of a Rescued Puppy.* New York: Collins, 2008.

Kaye, Cathryn Berger. *A Kids' Guide to Protecting & Caring for Animals: How to Take Action!* Minneapolis: Free Spirit, 2008.

Kehret, Peg. *Shelter Dogs: Amazing Stories of Adopted Strays.* Morton Grove, Ill.: Albert Whitman, 1999.

Larson, Kirby, Mary Nethery, and Jean Cassels. *Two Bobbies: A True Story of Hurricane Katrina, Friendship, and Survival.* New York: Walker, 2008.

Loeper, John J. *Crusade for Kindness: Henry Bergh and the ASPCA.* New York: Atheneum, 1991.

Miller-Schroeder, Patricia. *ASPCA.* Mankato, Minn.: Weigl, 2003.

Newkirk, Ingrid. *50 Awesome Ways Kids Can Help Animals: Fun and Easy Ways to Be a Kind Kid.* New York: Warner Books, 2006.

Spiotta-DiMare, Loren, Kara Lee, and the Humane Society of the United States. *Caesar: On Deaf Ears.* Fairfield, Conn.: Benefactory, 1997.

Suen, Anastasia. *The American Society for the Prevention of Cruelty to Animals.* New York: Powerkids Press, 2002.

Weil, Zoe, and John R. Gibson. *So, You Love Animals: An Action-Packed, Fun-Filled Book to Help Kids Help Animals.* Jenkintown, Pa.: Animalearn: American Anti-Vivisection Society, 1994.

Books for Older Readers and Adults

Arluke, Arnold. *Just a Dog: Understanding Animal Cruelty and Ourselves*. Philadelphia: Temple University Press, 2006.

Beers, Diane L. *For the Prevention of Cruelty: The History and Legacy of Animal Rights Activism in the United States*. Athens, Ohio: Swallow Press/Ohio University Press, 2006.

Brestrup, Craig. *Disposable Animals: Ending the Tragedy of Throwaway Pets*. Leander, Tex.: Camino Bay Books, 1997.

Coppinger, Raymond, and Lorna Coppinger. *Dogs: A Startling New Understanding of Canine Origin, Behavior, and Evolution*. New York: Scribner, 2001.

Derr, Mark. *A Dog's History of America: How Our Best Friend Explored, Conquered, and Settled a Continent*. New York: North Point Press, 2004.

Dodman, Nicholas H. *If Only They Could Speak: Stories About Pets and Their People*. New York: W. W. Norton, 2002.

Dye, Dan, and Mark Beckloff. *Amazing Gracie: A Dog's Tale*. New York: Workman, 2000.

Foster, Ken. *The Dogs Who Found Me: What I've Learned from Pets Who Were Left Behind*. Guilford, Conn.: Lyons Press, 2006.

———. *Dogs I Have Met: And the People They Found*. Guilford, Conn.: Lyons Press, 2008.

Grier, Katherine C. *Pets in America: A History*. Chapel Hill: University of North Carolina Press, 2006.

Lane, Marion S., and Stephen L. Zawistowski. *Heritage of Care: The American Society for the Prevention of Cruelty to Animals*. Westport, Conn.: Praeger, 2008.

Merck, Melinda. *Veterinary Forensics: Animal Cruelty Investigations*. Ames, Iowa: Blackwell, 2007.

Pace, Mildred Mastin, Danny L. Miller, and Paul Brown. *Friend of Animals: The Story of Henry Bergh*. Ashland, Ky.: Jesse Stuart Foundation, 1995.

Serpell, James. *The Domestic Dog: Its Evolution, Behaviour, and Interactions with People*. Cambridge, England, and New York: Cambridge University Press, 1995.

———. *In the Company of Animals: A Study of Human-Animal Relationships*. Cambridge, England, and New York: Cambridge University Press, 2003.

Sinclair, Leslie, Melinda Merck, and Randall Lockwood. *Forensic Investigation of Animal Cruelty: A Guide for Veterinary and Law Enforcement Professionals*. Washington, D.C.: Humane Society Press, 2006.

Swanbeck, Steve. *Disposable Dogs: Heartwarming, True Stories of Courage and Compassion*. Chester, N.J.: White Swan, 2004.

Thurston, Mary Elizabeth. *The Lost History of the Canine Race: Our 15,000-Year Love Affair with Dogs*. Kansas City, Mo.: Andrews and McMeel, 1996.

Williams, Erin E., and Margo DeMello. *Why Animals Matter: The Case for Animal Protection*. Amherst, N.Y.: Prometheus Books, 2007.

INTERNET RESOURCES

Today, you can easily find lots of general information about dog breeds, dog care, dog health, and just about anything else about dogs on the Internet. The American Society for the Prevention of Cruelty to Animals (www.aspca.org), The Humane Society of the United States (www.humanesociety.org), and other animal advocacy groups maintain excellent websites with an abundance of valuable information—everything from fostering dogs to selecting the right dog for your family to fighting puppy mills. The American Kennel Club (www.akc.org) provides information on registered breeds and their clubs, many of which support dog rescue efforts. Local animal shelters and breed rescues also have websites on which they feature adoptable pets, including photographs and adoption information. These websites are often linked to Petfinder (www.petfinder. com), which is one of the best ways to find an animal that needs a home. You can search by animal, breed, and location to find the perfect dog nearby. Searching these websites, networking on Facebook, and blogging about dog care can be excellent ways to learn more about dogs, check out volunteer opportunities, make charitable donations, and become involved in animal rescue at any age.

PHOTO CREDITS

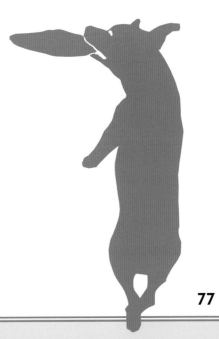

About the Author
AND HIS FAMILY DOGS

Raymond Bial (pronounced *Beal*) is the author and photo-illustrator of more than one hundred acclaimed books for children and adults, including *Amish Home*; *Frontier Home*; *The Underground Railroad*; *Tenement: Immigrant Life on the Lower East Side*; *Nauvoo: Mormon City on the Mississippi River*; and *Ellis Island: Coming to the Land of Liberty*. His books have received numerous awards from the American Library Association, the National Council of Teachers of English, the Children's Book Council, and many other organizations. His daughter Anna, who has illustrated two of his books, is a fashion designer in New York City. Raymond lives in Urbana, Illinois, with his wife, Linda, their children, Sarah and Luke, and their various pets.

For *Rescuing Rover*, Raymond managed to photograph for an entire day at the local shelter before adopting Isabel, a petite and demure Siamese cat. He and Linda now have a Siamese named Leo, four rescued dogs (Suzie, Zander, Lucky, and Boone), and Isabel, who actually considers herself an "honorary dog." She loves to hang out with the dogs, especially when treats are being handed out.

INDEX

Page numbers in *italics* refer to photo caption pages.

A

abandoned dogs, *8,* 9–10, *10–11, 31, 32, 35*
Abbie (former puppy mill dog), *28*
abused dogs
    criminal investigations, 38, 44, 46, 77
    neglected, *12, 32, 46. See also* puppy mills
    physically harmed, 32. *See also* dogfighting
adoption, 38, 56–57, *56–57,* 60–68, *61–69*
All Animals magazine, 39
American Kennel Club, 75
American Society for the Prevention of Cruelty to Animals (ASPCA)
    about, *36–38, 38,* 44, 76–77
    adoption van, *38*
    Advocacy Brigade, 28
    criminal investigations, 38, 46, 77
    dogs rescued by, *12, 14, 22–23, 25, 37, 68*
    New York City, *20–21, 36, 68, 76, 77*
    website, 75
    work to end puppy mills, *22–23,* 28
animal control officers, *9, 12, 44–45,* 44–46
Animal Precinct television show, *12, 45*
animal sanctuaries, 42
Animal Sheltering magazine, 39
animal shelters. *See also* rescue groups
    adoption from, 56–57, *56–57,* 60–68, *61–69*
    Champaign County, Ill., 43, *43, 50, 57*
    funding, 19, 35, 42, 43, 46
    life in, *20–21, 31, 50–56, 51–54*
    "no-kill" policy, 19, 42, 47
    number of cats and dogs per year, 19
    oldest in the U.S., 40
    "open-door" policy, 42, 43
    owner education, 40, 58, 66, 68
    percent of dogs in U.S. from, 19
    percent of dogs which are purebred, 30
    private, 42
    public, 40, *40*
    reasons dogs end up in, 32, 35
    staff. *See* animal shelter workers; volunteers
    veterinary care at, 40, *51–52, 52, 59, 67, 76*
animal shelter workers, 58–59, *59,* 64, 65
assistance dogs, 16

B

Bergh, Henry, 38
Best Friends Animal Sanctuary, 42
Bial, Linda, *8,* 10, 78, *78–79*
Bial, Raymond, 10, 78, *78–79*
bites, 44
Boone (author's dog), 10, *69, 79*
breeders, responsible vs. irresponsible, 22–23, 28
breeding
    diseases from inferior, 27
    history, 16, *16, 19*
    puppy mills and backyard, *22–28,* 22–30, 39
Butch (pit bull), *19*

D

disasters, animal rescue due to, *35, 39,* 76
dogfighting, 32, 35, *35,* 39
"dog pounds," 40. *See also* animal shelters
dogs
    number in the U.S., 15
    number "put down" per year, 12
    percent of households with, 15
    shared history with humans, 10–11, 15–16, *16, 19*
domestication, 16

E

Echo Dogs White Shepherd Rescue, 47
euthanized animals, 12, 19. *See also* "no-kill" policy
evolution, 15–16

F

farm animals and livestock, 39, 42, *46,* 77
finding a dog to own
    adoption from a shelter, 56–57, *56–57,* 60–68, *61–69*
    avoid pet stores, 23, 25, 28
    newspaper ad, 56
    online. *See* Internet
    rescue groups, 30, 57
    research as first step, 61
finding a lost dog, 44
fishing dogs, 16
foster homes, 10, 47, 48–49, *49*
Freddie (former puppy mill dog), *24*

G

Gankiewicz, Officer Adam, *12*
guard dogs, 16
guide dogs, 16

H

hearing dogs, 16
herding dogs, 16
history
    ASPCA, *36–38, 38,* 44
    of dogs and humans, 10–11, 15–16, *16, 19*
    HSUS, 39, *39*
    oldest animal shelter, 40
    puppy mills, 28
homes, finding
    adoption policies, 60
    difficult to place breeds, 19, 35
    difficult to place dogs, 19, *30, 35,* 42, *58*
    foster home until forever home, 48–49, *49*
Humane Society of the United States (HSUS)
    dogs rescued by, *32, 35*
    history, 39, *39*
    Humane Wildlife Services, 39
    magazines, 39
    website, 75
    work to end puppy mills, 28, *35,* 39
hunting dogs, 16, *16*

I

illness and disease, 27, 32, 52, 67
Internet, 10, 28, 30, *56, 57,* 75
Isabel (author's cat), 10, *78,* 78

K

Kristi (newly adopted dog), 68

L

legislation, 28, 39, 40, 46, 68, 77
LeKostaj, Ellen, 58–59
Leo (author's cat), 10, *78*
livestock. *See* farm animals and livestock
Lucas, Officer Annemarie, *45*
Lucky (author's dog), 10, *79*

M

microchip and ID tag, 68

N

"no-kill" policy, 19, 42, 47

O

"open-door" policy, 42, 43

overpopulation, 12, 19, 22, 32, 56
owners
    education, 40, 44, 58, 66, 68
    responsible vs. irresponsible, 32, 35

P

Petfinder.com, 10, *56, 57,* 75
pets other than dogs, 19, 46, *46*
pet stores, 23, 25, 28
placement. *See* homes, finding
puppy mills, abuse in, *22–28,* 22–30, 39
"put to sleep." *See* euthanized animals

R

rescue groups
    about, *46,* 46–47
    adoption from, *24,* 30, 57
    "no-kill" policy, 19, 42, 47
    resources, information, 70–73, 75
rodent control, 16

S

service dogs, 16
show dogs, 19, 22
sled dogs, 16, 19
spayed or neutered dogs, 19, 40, *52, 53,* 60, 76
Suzie (author's dog), *8,* 9–10, *10–11, 69, 78–79*
Suzy (newly adopted dog), 68

T

Tails Humane Society, 51
therapy dogs, 16
training, behavioral, *35,* 40, 48, 59, 76

V

volunteers
    animal shelter, 40, 51, 53–54, *54, 57*
    foster home, 48–49
    HSUS, 32
    rescue group, 46

W

Wally (foster home dog), *49*
wildlife, 39, *39,* 40, 42, 44
wolves, domestication, 15–16
working dogs. *See* herding dogs; hunting dogs

Z

Zander (author's dog), 10, *79*